LIGHTNING BOLT BOOKS™

Labrador Retrievers

Sarah Frank

Lerner Publications • Minneapolis

Lerner Publications Company
A division of Lerner Publishing Group, Inc.
241 First Avenue North
Minneapolis, MN 55401 USA

For reading levels and more information, look up this title at www.lernerbooks.com.

Library of Congress Cataloging-in-Publication Data

Names: Frank, Sarah, author.
Title: Labrador retrievers / Sarah Frank.
Description: Minneapolis : Lerner Publications, [2019] | Series: Lightning bolt books. Who's a good dog? | Audience: Age 6-9. | Audience: Grade K to 3. | Includes bibliographical references and index.
Identifiers: LCCN 2018004397 | ISBN 9781541538566 (lb : alk. paper)
Subjects: LCSH: Labrador retriever—Juvenile literature.
Classification: LCC SF429.L3 F73 2019 | DDC 636.752/7—dc23

LC record available at https://lccn.loc.gov/2018004397

Manufactured in the United States of America
1-45039-35866-6/4/2018

Table of Contents

The Perfect Dog

Picture the perfect dog. Is it sweet? Maybe it's playful or supersmart. Or maybe you want a dog that's all of these things. Then you might want a Labrador retriever!

Labrador retrievers are called Labs for short. These dogs are big bundles of love! They weigh from 55 to 80 pounds (25 to 36 kg). They grow to about 2 feet (0.6 m) tall at the shoulder.

Labs can be black, yellow, or chocolate brown.

Labs love the water.

Labs are ready for fun when you are. Take your Lab for a walk. Play fetch. Teach your dog new tricks.

Many families choose Labs as pets. They are great with kids and adults. They do well around other pets. But most of all, Labs love being with their owners.

Aw, puppy love!

All about Labs

There are so many kinds of dogs! The American Kennel Club (AKC) groups dogs by type. One of the AKC's groups is the sporting group. Labs are in this group.

Sporting dogs are active.
They need lots of exercise.
They do well in both the
water and the woods.

Do you think he's doing
the doggy paddle?

Labs are from Canada. In the nineteenth century, British travelers to Canada saw the Labs and loved them. They brought some back to Britain. Then American visitors to Britain brought some to the United States.

Labs in Canada helped fishers by pulling in their fishing nets.

Labs are purebreds. That means a Lab's parents are both Labs too. Owners of purebreds often register them with the AKC. More Labs are registered with the AKC than any other breed.

Should You Get a Lab?

Labs are awesome. But they aren't for everyone. Families should decide together if a Lab is right for them.

Labs are large. Lots of people like a huge pooch. But large dogs need space. Do you have room for a Lab?

Loving a Lab means giving it space to stretch out.

Labs also need tons of attention. They shouldn't be alone for long. Lonely Labs might misbehave!

Big dogs are big eaters. Feeding a Lab can be costly. Talk this over with an adult in your family. Can you afford a big dog?

Doggy Basics

Maybe you decided that a Lab's the pooch for you. That's great! Now it's time to get a few supplies. Think collar, leash, toys, and dog food.

Next to you, the vet may be your Lab's new BFF!

You'll also want to get your Lab to a vet. The vet will check your Lab for health problems. And your dog will get the shots it needs to stay healthy.

All dogs need to be groomed.
But Labs do not need tons of
grooming. You should brush
it now and then, though. This
helps remove dead skin and fur.

Brushing
time can be
bonding time!

Your Lab will look to you for love and care. Don't let it down! Dogs need attention even when you're tired or busy. A happy, healthy Lab will bring you years of joy.

How cute is that?!

Doggone Good Tips!

Looking for a name for your new Lab? Here are some ideas: Astro, Harley, Goldie (for a yellow Lab), Velvet (for a black Lab), or Cocoa (for a chocolate brown Lab).

Retrieve means "to bring something back." And Labs are very good at retrieving. These dogs can spend hours playing fetch!

Lab puppies are cute, but they shouldn't come home with you right away. They need to stay with their mom for eight weeks to learn from her and nurse, or drink her milk.

Why Labs Are the Best

- One has his very own movie. Ever hear of Marley? He was a real-life Lab made famous by the books his owner wrote about him. One of the books was made into a film. Marley's popularity only went up after his film came out.

- Labs are the perfect size for petting! You won't have to kneel to pet this big pooch.

- Labs have webbed feet. Not too many pooches have feet like that! The feet make Labs great at swimming.

Glossary

American Kennel Club (AKC): an organization that groups dogs by breed

breed: a particular type of dog. Dogs of the same breed have the same body shape and general features.

groom: to clean, brush, and trim a dog's coat

purebred: a dog whose parents are both of the same breed

register: to enter or sign up with an official group

sporting group: a group of dogs that are active, alert, and known for performing well outdoors and in the water

vet: a doctor who treats animals

Further Reading

American Kennel Club
http://www.akc.org

American Society for the Prevention of Cruelty to Animals
https://www.aspca.org

Barnes, Nico. *Labrador Retrievers*. Minneapolis: Abdo Kids, 2015.

Boothroyd, Jennifer. *Hero Service Dogs*. Minneapolis: Lerner Publications, 2017.

Gray, Susan H., and Maria Koran. *Labradors*. New York: AV2 by Weigl, 2018.

Index

Photo Acknowledgments

Image credits: Eric Isselee/Shutterstock.com, pp. 2, 4, 12; claire norman/Shutterstock.com, p. 5; Ben Birchall/PA Images/Getty Images, p. 6; Westend61/Getty Images, p. 7; Mos-Photography/Getty Images, p. 8; 3bugsmom/Getty Images, p. 9; Mark Raycroft/Minden Pictures/Getty Images, p. 10; THEPALMER/Getty Images, p. 11; Jaromir Chalabala/Shutterstock.com, p. 13; Africa Studio/Shutterstock.com, pp. 14, 15; Lleistock/Shutterstock.com, p. 16; Wallace and Wyant/The Image Bank/Getty Images, p. 17; Dorling Kindersley/Getty Images, p. 18; Ryan McVay/Stockbyte/Getty Images, p. 19; Dmitry Kalinovsky/Shutterstock.com, p. 23.

Cover: Eric Isselee/Shutterstock.com.

Main body text set in Billy Infant regular 28/36. Typeface provided by SparkType.